5-3-18

Love, Mom

The Bride's Essential
Mini 411
Checklists, Calendars, Contacts

Amy Nebens

D0733758

Sterling Signature
NEW YORK

Sterling Signature
NEW YORK

An Imprint of Sterling Publishing
387 Park Avenue South
New York, NY 10016

This edition published in 2013 by Sterling Publishing Co., Inc.

ISBN 978-1-4549-0842-5

Distributed in Canada by Sterling Publishing
c/o Canadian Manda Group, 165 Dufferin Street
Toronto, Ontario, Canada M6K 3H6
Distributed in the United Kingdom by GMC Distribution Services
Castle Place, 166 High Street, Lewes, East Sussex, England BN7 1XU
Distributed in Australia by Capricorn Link (Australia) Pty. Ltd.
P.O. Box 704, Windsor, NSW 2756, Australia

For information about custom editions, special sales, and premium and
corporate purchases, please contact Sterling Special Sales at 800-805-5489
or specialsales@sterlingpublishing.com.

Manufactured in China

6   8   10   9   7

www.sterlingpublishing.com

How to Use This Book

The Bride's Essential Mini 411 has been designed to help you stay on top of your wedding planning no matter where you are. Thanks to its compact size, you can easily keep it in your purse, so that you'll have valuable information with you at all times.

In the pages that follow, you'll find ready-made checklists to help you keep up with the many things you need to do as you're out and about. Each checklist covers a specific aspect of a wedding and the events surrounding it. Note that individual circumstances vary, so not all of the steps in those checklists will necessarily apply to your celebration. Simply use these lists according to your needs. And, since you'll undoubtedly have preparations particular to your own situation that aren't included here, there are blank checklists for you to jot down your own to-do notes.

This book also provides monthly calendar grids for keeping track of appointments with vendors, as well as space to record the addresses and phone numbers of people playing an important role in your wedding. It's easy to become overwhelmed by all of the elements that go into planning the big day, but staying organized and keeping key information in an easily accessible place will be a big help.

Contents

Checklists

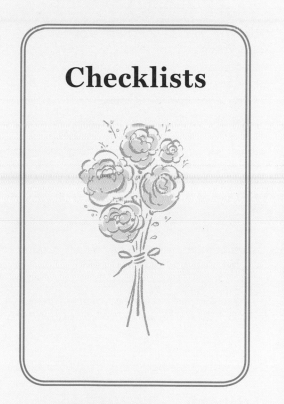

Planning Overview

Following is a general overview of the steps involved in planning a wedding. Keep in mind that locations, service providers, even officiants can be booked up more than a year in advance. While the schedule below can be used as a guide for budgeting your time, the earlier you make arrangements, the better. And, of course, if certain elements of the wedding are bigger priorities for you than others, you may want to focus on them first.

Nine Months Before or Earlier

☐ Arrange get-together for families to meet, celebrate, and discuss wedding plans

☐ Announce engagement in newspapers

☐ Discuss budget—with each other and family (include both families in talks if both families will be contributing financially)

☐ Pick a date—and alternative ones so you can be flexible when it comes to the availability of a venue or a wedding professional you want to hire

☐ Go for engagement photograph sitting

☐ Hire wedding consultant

☐ Select attendants, and ask them to be members of your wedding party

- ☐ Compile guest list
- ☐ Book site for ceremony
- ☐ Book site for reception
- ☐ Book officiant
- ☐ Hire caterer
- ☐ Hire musicians for ceremony
- ☐ Hire band/disc jockey for reception
- ☐ Order dress, veil, and headpiece

Six to Nine Months Before

- ☐ Hire photographer
- ☐ Hire videographer
- ☐ Book florist
- ☐ Select and order attendants' dresses and accessories
- ☐ Reserve rental equipment, including tent, tables, chairs, linens, china, and any other desired items
- ☐ Meet with caterer to plan menu and schedule tasting
- ☐ Order invitations and other wedding stationery
- ☐ Book calligrapher
- ☐ Mail save-the-date cards to out-of-town guests
- ☐ If having an at-home wedding, begin any necessary home improvements and/or landscaping work
- ☐ Hold block of hotel rooms for out-of-town guests
- ☐ Reserve your room for wedding night

- ☐ Look into potential honeymoon destinations and travel arrangements
- ☐ If traveling abroad, update passports, visas, and any other required travel documents and inquire about necessary immunizations
- ☐ Register for wedding gifts

Four to Six Months Before

- ☐ Make final honeymoon reservations
- ☐ Purchase/order/make favors
- ☐ Schedule time for ceremony rehearsal
- ☐ Plan rehearsal dinner (whether this involves making the arrangements yourself or discussing the event with the groom's family)
- ☐ Purchase tuxedo/suit, or reserve rental (groom and groomsmen)
- ☐ Meet with florist to discuss and decide upon bouquets, arrangements, etc.
- ☐ Order wedding cake (and groom's cake, if desired)
- ☐ Buy/order/make gifts for bridal party
- ☐ Purchase bridal shoes and other accessories
- ☐ Have invitations addressed

Two to Four Months Before

- [ ] Mail hotel, transportation, and area attractions information to out-of-town guests (if wedding is in a popular tourist destination during peak season, you may want to do this earlier)
- [ ] Plan post-wedding brunch
- [ ] Investigate local requirements for obtaining marriage license
- [ ] Book/arrange for transportation for bride, groom, attendants, and immediate family on wedding day
- [ ] Meet with officiant to discuss service
- [ ] If writing your own vows, begin doing so now
- [ ] Select readings/songs for ceremony; ask those you want to read/perform if they will do the honor
- [ ] Make selections for ceremony music
- [ ] Choose songs for the major highlights of reception (first dance, cake-cutting, bouquet toss, etc.)
- [ ] Buy appropriate undergarments and hosiery for wedding gown, and bring to first fitting
- [ ] Purchase wedding rings
- [ ] Select gift for groom, if you two are exchanging presents
- [ ] Select thank-you gifts for parents
- [ ] Purchase going-away outfit
- [ ] Send invitations (this should be done six to eight weeks before wedding)

- ☐ Inquire about local newspapers' time requirements and content guidelines for wedding announcements
- ☐ Sit for wedding portrait
- ☐ Do trial runs with makeup artist and hairstylist, and schedule beauty appointments for the wedding day

Four to Six Weeks Before
- ☐ Make arrangements for blood tests, if state requires (check with the local town clerk's office to find out if and when exactly this needs to be done)
- ☐ Obtain marriage license (the time period during which this needs to be done varies according to local regulations; check with the local town clerk's office)
- ☐ Create/order ceremony programs
- ☐ Plan bridesmaids' luncheon
- ☐ Put together welcome baskets for out-of-town guests
- ☐ Send wedding announcements to newspapers
- ☐ Give list of songs you want (and don't want) played to band/disc jockey
- ☐ Have final dress fitting
- ☐ Pick up ordered tuxedo/suit, if purchasing (groom and groomsmen)
- ☐ Start arranging seating plan
- ☐ Pick up wedding rings

Two Weeks Before

- [ ] Provide caterer with final head count
- [ ] Finalize seating plan; write place cards, or give calligrapher the information and materials to do so
- [ ] Send shot lists to photographer and videographer
- [ ] Compose toasts for rehearsal dinner and wedding reception
- [ ] Make a detailed schedule of the wedding reception events (times for cocktails, first dance, dinner, cake-cutting, etc.) to give to all applicable service providers
- [ ] Break in shoes and scuff bottoms

One Week Before

- [ ] Pick up dress, if not being delivered
- [ ] Pick up tuxedo, if renting (groom and groomsmen)
- [ ] Confirm reservations for wedding night and honeymoon
- [ ] Obtain crisp bills from bank for gratuities; put tips in labeled envelopes and seal
- [ ] Organize final payments for service providers who need to be paid on wedding day
- [ ] Pack for honeymoon
- [ ] Purchase traveler's checks for honeymoon
- [ ] Make a list of everything you need to bring to wedding, and gather all the necessary items together
- [ ] Host bridesmaids' luncheon (often done the day before

the wedding to accommodate out-of-town attendants)
- [ ] Confirm final details with all service providers
- [ ] Arrange for mail to be held at post office and newspaper to be put on hold.
- [ ] Instruct stores where you're registered to hold deliveries

One Day Before

- [ ] Drop off welcome baskets for out-of-town guests at hotel (or ask attendant to do so)
- [ ] Get manicure and pedicure
- [ ] Have rehearsal; hand out gifts to wedding party if you haven't already done so
- [ ] Assign tasks and duties to wedding party for next day
- [ ] Give attendants anything they need to execute said duties
- [ ] Attend rehearsal dinner
- [ ] Give groom his gift, if you two are exchanging presents (could be done on wedding night instead)

Ceremony: Setting the Stage

- [ ] Schedule appointments with site coordinators and/or officiants
- [ ] Check out potential ceremony venues in person
- [ ] Book site for ceremony
- [ ] Send signed contract and deposit for ceremony site
- [ ] Book officiant
- [ ] Ask desired friends and/or family members to be your attendants
- [ ] Be sure to comply with any restrictions that the ceremony site and officiant have regarding music, attire, photography, videography, decorations, or anything else when making plans
- [ ] Reserve any necessary rental items
- [ ] Schedule rehearsal (be sure to clear time with all participants)
- [ ] Set times for any necessary meetings/counseling sessions with officiant
- [ ] Make arrangements for ceremony music (see page 31)
- [ ] Arrange to have flowers for ceremony (see page 30)
- [ ] Make arrangements for any other decorations for ceremony site

- ☐ Contact local town clerk's office to find out marriage license requirements:
  - ☐ how far in advance you need to and are able to obtain license
  - ☐ what jurisdiction license needs to be from (i.e. where you'll be married or where you live)
  - ☐ what the fee is and what type of payment is accepted
  - ☐ whether there are any witness requirements
  - ☐ whether a blood test is required, what must be tested for, and where you can get the appropriate test
- ☐ Get blood tests, if required (do so within appropriate time frame according to local regulations)
- ☐ Obtain marriage license (do so within appropriate time frame according to local regulations)
- ☐ Acquire any necessary official religious documents
- ☐ Arrange for place to get dressed before ceremony
- ☐ Other _____
- ☐ _____
- ☐ _____
- ☐ _____

Ceremony: Contents

- ☐ Plan/write vows
- ☐ Plan/adapt/review other parts of ceremony
- ☐ Choose readings and/or songs for special ceremony participants
- ☐ Send selected readings and/or songs to appropriate participants
- ☐ Acquire any objects needed to perform ceremony customs, such as drinking wine from a shared goblet, lighting the unity candle, or breaking the glass
- ☐ Purchase/make pillow for ring bearer; purchase basket and flower petals for girl(s)
- ☐ Make any desired seating arrangements
- ☐ Decide where to stage receiving line, if you choose to have one (could be done at reception site instead)
- ☐ Purchase birdseed/bubbles/rose petals for guests to shower you with as you leave ceremony site (this custom could instead be performed as you depart from the reception)
- ☐ Other _____
- ☐ _____
- ☐ _____
- ☐ _____
- ☐ _____

Ceremony: Final Details

☐ Make arrangements for distribution of ceremony programs and signing of guest book

☐ Determine order of attendants for processional

☐ Assign maid of honor or another attendant to arrange train and/or veil at altar

☐ Assign maid of honor or another attendant to hold your bouquet and/or glove during ceremony

☐ If no ring bearer, or ring bearer is just to carry bride's ring, assign maid of honor or another attendant to hold groom's ring during ceremony

☐ Assemble emergency supply kit for wedding day (see page 46 for contents)

☐ Arrange for a place to keep emergency kit during ceremony (and reception)

☐ Confirm final details/times with site coordinator and officiant

☐ Obtain contact numbers for site coordinator and officiant for wedding day

☐ Other _____

☐ _____

☐ _____

☐ _____

☐ _____

Reception: Setting the Stage

- [ ] Schedule appointments with site managers
- [ ] Schedule appointments with caterers, if necessary
- [ ] Hire wedding consultant (optional; see page 21)
- [ ] Check out potential reception sites in person
- [ ] Book reception venue
- [ ] Send signed contract and deposit for venue
- [ ] Interview potential caterers (if off-site)
- [ ] Hire caterer
- [ ] Send signed contract and deposit to caterer
- [ ] Make appointment for menu tasting
- [ ] Take care of necessary home improvements/landscaping issues, if having at-home wedding
- [ ] Make arrangements for reception music (see page 32)
- [ ] Make arrangements for floral decorations (see page 30)
- [ ] Arrange for other reception decorations
- [ ] Make menu selections
- [ ] Go to rentals showroom to look at chairs, tables, linens, china, etc.
- [ ] Reserve rental items
- [ ] Schedule delivery and pickup of rental items
- [ ] Schedule appointments/cake tastings with cake designers, if necessary
- [ ] Place order for wedding cake (and groom's cake, if desired)

- [ ] Select cake topper
- [ ] Make arrangements for guest parking, if necessary
- [ ] Other _____
- [ ] _____
- [ ] _____
- [ ] _____
- [ ] _____
- [ ] _____
- [ ] _____
- [ ] _____
- [ ] _____

Reception: Final Details

- [ ] Make arrangements for special cake-cutting knife
- [ ] Make arrangements for special toasting glasses for you and groom
- [ ] Arrange for place to store and change into going-away outfits
- [ ] Provide caterer and/or site coordinator with final head count
- [ ] Organize seating chart
- [ ] Compose toasts (from you to your groom; from the two of you thanking your hosts and guests)

- ☐ Confirm with rental company all details, dates, times, and site(s) where items must be delivered/picked up
- ☐ Obtain phone number of rental company contact for wedding day
- ☐ Confirm details with caterer
- ☐ Obtain phone number of caterer for wedding day
- ☐ Review timetable for all reception "events" (cocktails, first dance, dinner, cake-cutting, etc.) with caterer/site coordinator, and give this schedule to applicable service providers (photographer, videographer, band/disc jockey)
- ☐ Obtain phone number of site coordinator for day of wedding
- ☐ Give site coordinator arrival times for all service providers
- ☐ Give cake topper to cake designer/banquet manager, if you've obtained from a different source
- ☐ Give cake-cutting knife and toasting glasses to site coordinator/caterer
- ☐ Ask caterer/site coordinator to have top tier of wedding cake packed up for you (to save for first anniversary)
- ☐ Ask caterer/site coordinator to have cake topper packed up for you, if yours to keep
- ☐ Inform caterer/site coordinator of any cake-related elements that must be returned to cake designer, if applicable

- ☐ Arrange for friend or family member to return any items that must go back to cake designer, if applicable
- ☐ Ask friend or family member to take top tier of wedding cake home and freeze for you—and to take cake topper home, if applicable
- ☐ Arrange to have groom's cake cut up and boxed for favors, if desired
- ☐ Make arrangements to have some food packed up for you and groom to enjoy later, in case you don't eat much during the party
- ☐ Rope off any "off-limits" areas, if having an at-home wedding
- ☐ Put away any breakables or valuable items, if having an at-home wedding
- ☐ Other _____
- ☐ _____
- ☐ _____
- ☐ _____
- ☐ _____
- ☐ _____
- ☐ _____
- ☐ _____
- ☐ _____

Wedding Consultant

- [ ] Schedule appointments to interview candidates
- [ ] Hire wedding consultant
- [ ] Send signed contract and deposit to wedding consultant
- [ ] Schedule progress meetings
- [ ] Confirm final details with wedding consultant
- [ ] Obtain contact number of wedding consultant for wedding day
- [ ] Other _____
- [ ] _____
- [ ] _____
- [ ] _____
- [ ] _____
- [ ] _____
- [ ] _____

Stationery

- ☐ Discuss ideas and costs with stationers
- ☐ Search online for invitations and designs
- ☐ If DIY-ing, start thinking of designs and gathering materials
- ☐ Place order for desired stationery items (invitations, announcements, ceremony programs, etc.)
- ☐ Send deposit to stationer
- ☐ Provide stationer with final wording for invitation (and for any other items you're ordering)
- ☐ Review proofs for invitation and for any other applicable items
- ☐ Compile list of names (with correct spellings) and addresses for all invitees
- ☐ Meet with calligraphers to see work and discuss fees for any services you want (addressing invitations, doing table number cards and seating cards, etc.)
- ☐ Hire calligrapher, or recruit a talented friend for your calligraphy needs
- ☐ Send list of guests and addresses, along with envelopes, to person addressing invitations
- ☐ Send seating cards and/or table number cards—along with list of seating assignments—to calligrapher, if applicable

- ☐ Take a completely assembled invitation (with all its inserts and envelopes) to post office to determine necessary postage
- ☐ Buy special postage stamps for invitation envelopes and response envelopes
- ☐ Assemble invitations and stuff envelopes
- ☐ Take assembled invitations to post office to have them hand-canceled, and mail
- ☐ Purchase guest book
- ☐ Purchase pens for guest book (be sure to buy extras)
- ☐ Follow up with invitees who haven't responded (about two weeks before wedding)
- ☐ Address wedding announcements
- ☐ Ask family member or attendant to send wedding announcements on the day of or the day after the wedding
- ☐ Other _____
- ☐ _____
- ☐ _____
- ☐ _____
- ☐ _____
- ☐ _____
- ☐ _____
- ☐ _____
- ☐ _____

Bridal Attire: Part I

☐ Collect photos of dresses you admire from magazines and/or peruse online for styles you like
☐ Think about your theme and location as these can sometimes inspire a look
☐ Schedule appointments at bridal salons
☐ Invite parent, maid of honor, or other bridal attendant to go.to bridal salons with you
☐ Select:
  ☐ gown
  ☐ veil
  ☐ headpiece
  ☐ shoes (before first fitting)
  ☐ undergarments appropriate for gown (before first fitting)
  ☐ hosiery (have extra pairs on hand on wedding day)
  ☐ garter
  ☐ jewelry
  ☐ hair accessories
  ☐ purse
  ☐ wrap
  ☐ gloves
  ☐ going-away outfit
  ☐ rehearsal dinner outfit

- ☐ Make appointments for gown fittings and inquire as to what you will need to bring with you
- ☐ Obtain swatches of gown to give to florist and, if applicable, for professional who will be dyeing shoes

If borrowing a gown:

- ☐ Take gown out of storage
- ☐ Try on gown to determine what alterations, if any, are necessary
- ☐ Examine gown for stains and rips
- ☐ Take gown to reputable seamstress for alterations (if an older gown, take to a professional experienced in working with vintage garments)
- ☐ Take gown to reputable professional for cleaning and/or steaming

If renting a gown:

- ☐ Search online and locally for salons who rent gowns
- ☐ Get references
- ☐ Schedule appointments
- ☐ Find out alteration policy
- ☐ Ask about length of rental
- ☐ Inquire about a policy for return conditions
- ☐ Ask if others can rent the dress before your wedding after you've placed a deposit

☐ Other _____

☐ _____

Bridal Attire: Part II

- ☐ Have parent, maid of honor, or other bridal attendant accompany you to fitting in order to learn how to bustle train
- ☐ Obtain instructions from bridal salon on how to hang and care for dress
- ☐ Find out from bridal salon what to do if dress gets wrinkled before wedding
- ☐ Obtain instructions from bridal salon regarding spot/stain removal
- ☐ Determine time and place to bustle gown and remove or change headpiece after ceremony
- ☐ Have shoes dyed to match gown
- ☐ Pick up dyed shoes
- ☐ Pick up gown
- ☐ Break in shoes and scuff shoe bottoms by wearing them around the house (so that they're comfortable and you don't slip in them)
- ☐ Find professional dry cleaner who specializes in bridal gown care to clean and pack up dress and accessories after wedding
- ☐ Ask parent, attendant, or close friend to take bridal gown home for you after wedding (if you won't be able to do so yourself)

- [ ] Ask parent, attendant, or close friend to take gown to designated dry cleaner after wedding
- [ ] Other _____
- [ ] _____
- [ ] _____

Bridal Attendants' Attire

- [ ] Peruse magazines and online resources to check out different styles—be sure to look at bridesmaids' dresses as well as other dresses, such as cocktail, evening, and daytime. Consider your location, theme, and color scheme when looking
- [ ] Schedule appointments to shop for bridesmaid dresses
- [ ] Select dresses, or give attendants guidelines for choosing their own
- [ ] If attendants are selecting their own dresses in a color of your choosing, send them swatches of the color
- [ ] Give salon the appropriate measurements for your attendants, or have attendants do so
- [ ] Provide salon with any necessary contact information for attendants, or have attendants do so
- [ ] Check with salon to make sure that all bridesmaids have signed their contracts and that order has been placed, if applicable

- ☐ Arrange to have dresses sent to out-of-town attendants, or have attendants do so
- ☐ Obtain swatches of the bridesmaid dresses to show florist (for bouquets/arrangements) and professional who will be dyeing shoes
- ☐ Send swatches of bridesmaid dresses to attendants, if they will be responsible for having their shoes dyed
- ☐ If attendants are not all having alterations done at the same place, give them instructions as to where the hemline should fall
- ☐ Select attendants' shoes, or provide them with guidelines for doing so
- ☐ Pick out any accessories for attendants (purse, gloves, jewelry)
- ☐ Select attire for child attendants, or give their parents guidelines for doing so
- ☐ Check that attendants have their attire and accessories ready for the wedding day
- ☐ Other _____
- ☐ _____
- ☐ _____
- ☐ _____
- ☐ _____
- ☐ _____
- ☐ _____

Beauty Details

- [ ] Schedule appointment to try out hairstylist
- [ ] Schedule appointment to try out makeup artist
- [ ] Bring to trial run with hairstylist:
    - [ ] veil/headpiece
    - [ ] photo or sketch of dress to show neckline
    - [ ] photos of hairstyles you like
- [ ] Make appointment with hairstylist for wedding day
- [ ] Make appointment with makeup artist for wedding day
- [ ] Schedule appointment for manicure (and pedicure, if desired)
- [ ] Schedule appointments for bridesmaids and/or family members to have hair, makeup, and/or nails done, if desired
- [ ] Confirm all beauty appointments
- [ ] Wear a button-down shirt to hair and makeup appointments
- [ ] Obtain appropriate cosmetics for touch-ups during the wedding
- [ ] Other _____
- [ ] _____
- [ ] _____
- [ ] _____
- [ ] _____

Flowers

- ☐ Collect photos/magazine clippings of bouquets and flower arrangements to show florist what you like
- ☐ Schedule appointments to interview florists
- ☐ Book florist
- ☐ Schedule appointment to see sample bouquets and arrangements
- ☐ Give table sizes—for cocktails and reception—to florist (so that centerpieces can be sized accordingly)
- ☐ Supply florist with swatches of dresses/table linens (to achieve complementary bouquets/arrangements)
- ☐ Make selections for all desired floral items
- ☐ Send deposit to florist
- ☐ Send signed contract to florist
- ☐ Give measurement for length of aisle to florist if he/she is supplying runner
- ☐ Confirm final details with florist
- ☐ Confirm date, times, and locations with florist
- ☐ Obtain florist's contact number for wedding day
- ☐ Make arrangements for preservation of bouquet, if desired
- ☐ Other _____
- ☐ _____
- ☐ _____

- [ ] _____
- [ ] _____
- [ ] _____
- [ ] _____
- [ ] _____

Ceremony Music

- [ ] Interview ceremony musicians
- [ ] Make arrangements to listen to performances
- [ ] Hire ceremony musician(s)
- [ ] Send signed contract and deposit to musicians
- [ ] Choose music for:
    - [ ] prelude
    - [ ] attendants' processional
    - [ ] bride's processional
    - [ ] ceremony/interludes
    - [ ] recessional
    - [ ] postlude
- [ ] Provide musicians with any necessary sheet music
- [ ] Coordinate the logistics of musicians' setup with ceremony site
- [ ] Make any necessary arrangements for equipment required by musicians
- [ ] Coordinate timing of music with officiant and musicians

- ☐ Confirm date, times, place, and details with musicians
- ☐ Obtain contact numbers of musicians for wedding day
- ☐ Make a playlist on a digital music player for the rehearsal dinner or other pre-events to save on extra musician costs
- ☐ Other _____
- ☐ _____
- ☐ _____

Reception Music

- ☐ Interview bands or disc jockeys
- ☐ Listen to bands/disc jockeys perform
- ☐ Hire band/disc jockey
- ☐ Send signed contract and deposit to band/disc jockey
- ☐ Arrange to have music for:
  - ☐ cocktail hour
  - ☐ interlude between cocktail hour and main reception
  - ☐ introduction of married couple
  - ☐ first dance
  - ☐ father–daughter dance
  - ☐ mother–son dance
  - ☐ dinner
  - ☐ general dancing
  - ☐ traditional/religious dances

- [ ] cake-cutting
- [ ] bouquet toss
- [ ] bride and groom's exit
- [ ] Arrange for band/disc jockey to visit site and evaluate facilities for acoustics and electrical capabilities
- [ ] Provide band with sheet music for any songs you want them to learn
- [ ] Make any necessary arrangements for equipment required by band/disc jockey
- [ ] Coordinate arrangements as necessary with the reception site
- [ ] Sign up for dance lessons with groom, if desired
- [ ] Provide band/disc jockey with list of requested tunes and songs you don't want played
- [ ] Confirm date, times, and location with band/disc jockey
- [ ] Give schedule of reception events to band/disc jockey (include any announcements you want made, such as telling guests to pick up favors)
- [ ] Give any necessary music to disc jockey
- [ ] Obtain contact numbers of musicians/disc jockey for wedding day
- [ ] Other _____
- [ ] _____
- [ ] _____
- [ ] _____

Photography

- ☐ Peruse the wedding albums of friends and family to get a feel for different photography styles
- ☐ Schedule interviews with photographers
- ☐ Hire photographer
- ☐ Send signed contract and deposit to photographer
- ☐ Schedule sitting for engagement portrait
- ☐ Scout potential spots for photos—at home, at a local park, at the wedding location
- ☐ Select albums (including page and border style)
- ☐ Schedule sitting for wedding portrait, if announcing wedding in newspapers
- ☐ Purchase disposable cameras for guests' tables, if applicable
- ☐ Assign someone the task of placing disposable cameras on tables and collecting them at end of event
- ☐ Give photographer list of desired shots and important people to be photographed
- ☐ Assign attendant the responsibility of pointing out important people to photographer
- ☐ Provide said attendant with copy of shot list
- ☐ Confirm final details with photographer
- ☐ Confirm date, times, and locations with photographer
- ☐ Obtain contact number of photographer for wedding day

- [ ] Give photographer schedule of wedding day's events
- [ ] Other _____
- [ ] _____
- [ ] _____
- [ ] _____

Videography

- [ ] View wedding videos of family and friends to get acquainted with different styles
- [ ] Schedule interviews with videographers
- [ ] Hire videographer
- [ ] Send signed contract and deposit to videographer
- [ ] Provide videographer with list of desired shots and important people
- [ ] Assign attendant task of pointing out important people to videographer
- [ ] Provide said attendant with copy of shot list
- [ ] Confirm final details with videographer
- [ ] Confirm date, times, and locations with videographer
- [ ] Obtain contact number of videographer for wedding day
- [ ] Give videographer schedule of wedding day's events
- [ ] Other _____
- [ ] _____
- [ ] _____

Accommodations/Activities

- ☐ Make your hotel reservation for wedding night
- ☐ Hold block of hotel rooms for out-of-town guests
- ☐ Request special code for guests to use when booking rooms in the block
- ☐ Plan any desired group activities for your guests (e.g., a round-robin tennis tournament or an excursion to a nearby point of interest)
- ☐ Send hotel and transportation info to out-of-town guests; include directions from local airports and cities from which many guests will be driving, info regarding local attractions, and any code/name needed to receive discounted rate when making room reservations
- ☐ Assemble welcome baskets for guests' rooms
- ☐ Make any desired special arrangements for your wedding night (purchase lingerie, arrange to have chilled champagne waiting for you, etc.)
- ☐ Confirm your hotel reservation for wedding night
- ☐ Bring guest baskets to hotel, or assign someone to do so
- ☐ Other _____
- ☐ _____
- ☐ _____
- ☐ _____
- ☐ _____

Transportation

- ☐ Book/arrange for transportation for bride, groom, wedding party, and immediate family to ceremony and reception
- ☐ Book/arrange for bride and groom's post-reception getaway vehicle
- ☐ Book/arrange for transportation for immediate family and wedding party after reception
- ☐ Send signed contract and deposit for transportation
- ☐ Make arrangements for someone to drive bride's and/or groom's car(s) home after reception, if necessary
- ☐ Book shuttle service to take nonlocal guests from hotel to ceremony and reception and back to hotel, if desired
- ☐ Provide drivers with all necessary directions, addresses, and contact numbers
- ☐ Confirm all transportation arrangements
- ☐ Have any personal cars being used on wedding day washed so that they're nice and shiny for the event
- ☐ Fill bride's and/or groom's personal car(s) with plenty of gas, if being used on wedding day
- ☐ Other _____
- ☐ _____
- ☐ _____
- ☐ _____

Rehearsal Dinner

If groom's parents are planning the event:

- ☐ Discuss rehearsal dinner with groom's parents
- ☐ Provide groom's parents with the menu for the wedding reception so that the meals are not too similar
- ☐ Put together guest list for rehearsal dinner
- ☐ Give addresses or phone numbers of guests on your list to groom's parents
- ☐ Compose toast (with groom) to thank hosts and guests
- ☐ Other _____
- ☐ _____
- ☐ _____
- ☐ _____
- ☐ _____
- ☐ _____

If bride is involved in planning the event

- ☐ Book venue
- ☐ Send signed contract and deposit for venue
- ☐ Make selections for menu
- ☐ Arrange for decorations or music, if desired
- ☐ Make arrangements for entertainment (such as a slide show tracing the lives of you and your groom), if desired
- ☐ Put together guest list (with addresses, e-mails, or phone numbers) for rehearsal dinner

- ☐ Order/purchase/print out invitations, call invitees, or compose e-mail invitations
- ☐ Address invitations
- ☐ Send invitations
- ☐ Compose toast (with groom) to thank hosts and/or guests
- ☐ Give site manager final head count
- ☐ Confirm all details with site manager
- ☐ Other _____
- ☐ _____
- ☐ _____
- ☐ _____
- ☐ _____
- ☐ _____
- ☐ _____
- ☐ _____
- ☐ _____

Bridesmaids' Luncheon

- [ ] Prepare guest list
- [ ] Visit potential venues
- [ ] Reserve space
- [ ] Send deposit, if applicable
- [ ] Plan menu
- [ ] Have thank-you gifts for attendants—along with a personal note to each—ready for luncheon, if you plan to present them then (see page 45)
- [ ] Arrange for decorations for venue or table, if desired
- [ ] Order/purchase/create invitations, call invitees, or compose e-mail invitations
- [ ] Address invitations
- [ ] Send invitations
- [ ] Give final head count to site manager
- [ ] Confirm all details with venue
- [ ] Other _____
- [ ] _____
- [ ] _____
- [ ] _____
- [ ] _____
- [ ] _____
- [ ] _____
- [ ] _____

Post-Wedding Brunch

By no means a required event, this get-together can be hosted by anyone who wants to do so, from the bride and groom to their parents to relatives or family friends.

☐ Compile guest list

☐ Schedule appointments with site managers or caterers, if applicable

☐ Book site or caterer, depending on your needs

☐ Send deposit, if applicable

☐ Plan menu

☐ Order/purchase/create invitations, call invitees, or compose e-mail invitations

☐ Address invitations

☐ Send invitations

☐ Tally final guest count

☐ Give final head count to site/caterer, if applicable

☐ Confirm all arrangements

☐ Other _____

☐ _____

☐ _____

☐ _____

☐ _____

☐ _____

☐ _____

Rings

- ☐ Have engagement ring insured, if groom has not done so already
- ☐ Select wedding bands
- ☐ Pick up wedding bands from jeweler
- ☐ Have wedding bands engraved
- ☐ Pick up wedding bands from engraver
- ☐ Have engagement ring cleaned (so it gleams on your wedding day)
- ☐ Give wedding bands to honor attendants (best man holds on to bride's; maid of honor holds groom's)
- ☐ Other _____
- ☐ _____
- ☐ _____
- ☐ _____
- ☐ _____

Gift Registry

- ☐ Sign up for an online registry at any retailer site, or at a wedding site that will consolidate and cross-reference wedding gift purchases
- ☐ Call stores to find out whether you need to make an appointment to register
- ☐ Select potential times to go shopping with groom
- ☐ Make appointments with registry departments
- ☐ Register for gifts
- ☐ Check online to see if your wish list is in place and accurate
- ☐ Let your parents and attendants know where you have registered, so that they are prepared to respond when people ask
- ☐ Follow up with stores, in the event of an address change, as to where packages should be sent
- ☐ Other _____
- ☐ _____
- ☐ _____
- ☐ _____
- ☐ _____
- ☐ _____
- ☐ _____
- ☐ _____

Favors

☐ Purchase/order/make favors
☐ Compose any message you want to attach to favor
☐ Have message professionally printed, or do it yourself
☐ Assemble and wrap favors
☐ Decide how, where, and when to present favors (be sure to consult reception site manager)
☐ Determine who will set up favors at reception site
☐ Assign an attendant the task of bringing favors to reception site
☐ Set one favor aside for you and your groom as a keepsake
☐ Other _____
☐ _____
☐ _____
☐ _____
☐ _____
☐ _____
☐ _____
☐ _____
☐ _____
☐ _____
☐ _____
☐ _____

Gifts for Others

- [ ] Purchase/order/create presents for bridal attendants (groom should do same for groomsmen)
- [ ] Wrap gifts for bridal attendants (groom should do same for groomsmen's gifts)
- [ ] Purchase/order/create presents for child attendants
- [ ] Wrap presents for child attendants
- [ ] Purchase present for groom, if the two of you are exchanging gifts
- [ ] Buy thank-you gifts for parents
- [ ] Wrap groom's gift
- [ ] Wrap parents' presents
- [ ] Write personal notes to each bridesmaid, each child attendant, your parents, and if desired, your groom
- [ ] Decide when to present members of wedding party with their gifts
- [ ] Decide when to present groom with his gift, if applicable
- [ ] Decide when you'll give parents their presents
- [ ] Other _____
- [ ] _____
- [ ] _____
- [ ] _____
- [ ] _____
- [ ] _____

Bride's Emergency Kit

There are a number of items that you should have on hand at the ceremony and reception in case of attire and beauty "emergencies." Organize them into a small bag. Following are things you may want to include.

- ☐ Sewing kit
- ☐ Fabric tape (for a quick fix to a hem)
- ☐ Safety pins
- ☐ Corsage pins
- ☐ Extra earring backs
- ☐ Extra hosiery (in case of runs)
- ☐ Clear nail polish (for small runs)
- ☐ Chalk (to cover up any last minute wedding dress splotches)
- ☐ Spot remover
- ☐ Static cling spray
- ☐ Tweezers
- ☐ Makeup for touch-ups
- ☐ Mirror
- ☐ Facial tissues
- ☐ Blotting tissues
- ☐ Bobby pins
- ☐ Comb/hairbrush

- ☐ Dental floss/toothpicks
- ☐ Breath mints
- ☐ Headache relief medication
- ☐ Stomach medication
- ☐ Bandages
- ☐ Bottle of water
- ☐ Straws (to stay hydrated without smudging lipstick)
- ☐ Tampons/sanitary napkins
- ☐ Extra pair of contact lenses
- ☐ Rewetting solution for contact lenses

Gratuities

- ☐ Figure out gratuity amounts and obtain crisp bills from bank
- ☐ Put tips in labeled envelopes and seal
- ☐ Assign attendant/family member to hand out tips on wedding day, if host isn't distributing them
- ☐ Give tips to assigned person to hand out
- ☐ Other _____
- ☐ _____
- ☐ _____
- ☐ _____
- ☐ _____

Honeymoon

☐ Ask friends and family for honeymoon destination recommendations

☐ Meet with a travel agent/tour operator specializing in chosen destination, if not making the arrangements yourself

☐ Research potential destinations and hotels

☐ Arrange to take time off from work for honeymoon

☐ Book transportation to destination

☐ Make hotel reservations

☐ If renting a car, find out if your automobile insurance covers you on a rental car in the honeymoon location or if you should purchase insurance from the rental company

☐ Book car rental/transportation between airport and hotel at destination, if necessary

☐ Update travel documents (passports, visas, etc.), if they're not current and you're traveling out of the country

☐ Obtain travel insurance, if desired

☐ Acquire guidebooks about destination

☐ Acquire foreign language books/lesson programs, if applicable

☐ Get any necessary immunizations for foreign travel

☐ Book activities

- ☐ Make any desired dining reservations
- ☐ Buy any items needed for trip
- ☐ Arrange for transportation to airport for departure and from airport for return home
- ☐ Pick up tickets/itinerary from travel agent, if not being sent to you
- ☐ Obtain traveler's checks
- ☐ Change currency, if necessary
- ☐ Pack (include any special gear required for planned activities)
- ☐ Ask a reliable friend or family member to hold on to tickets/travel documents so they don't get lost in the wedding mayhem
- ☐ Confirm all reservations
- ☐ Arrange to have someone water your plants and/or take care of your pets, if necessary
- ☐ Arrange to have mail held at post office and newspaper delivery put on hold
- ☐ Instruct stores where you're registered to hold deliveries
- ☐ Give all of your contact information to a relative or friend in case of emergency
- ☐ Other _____
- ☐ _____
- ☐ _____
- ☐ _____

Beyond "I Do"

- [ ] Pick up held mail at post office, upon return from honeymoon
- [ ] Instruct stores where you've registered to resume gift delivery, upon return from honeymoon
- [ ] Fill out the appropriate paperwork to change name legally, if applicable
- [ ] Inform the appropriate agencies/businesses of name and/or address change, if applicable:
  - [ ] Department of Motor Vehicles
  - [ ] passport office
  - [ ] Social Security Administration
  - [ ] insurance agencies
  - [ ] credit card companies
  - [ ] banks/financial institutions
  - [ ] payroll offices
  - [ ] registrar of voters
- [ ] Contact any agencies/businesses that require knowledge of or should know about your change in marital status
- [ ] Send outstanding thank-you notes
- [ ] Mail change-of-address cards
- [ ] Call photographer to check on status of proofs
- [ ] Make follow-up call to videographer

☐ Other _____
☐ _____
☐ _____
☐ _____
☐ _____
☐ _____
☐ _____
☐ _____
☐ _____
☐ _____

Things to Do

- [ ] _____
- [ ] _____
- [ ] _____
- [ ] _____
- [ ] _____
- [ ] _____
- [ ] _____
- [ ] _____
- [ ] _____
- [ ] _____
- [ ] _____
- [ ] _____

Notes

_____
_____
_____
_____
_____
_____
_____
_____
_____
_____

Things to Do

- [ ] _____
- [ ] _____
- [ ] _____
- [ ] _____
- [ ] _____
- [ ] _____
- [ ] _____
- [ ] _____
- [ ] _____
- [ ] _____
- [ ] _____
- [ ] _____

Notes

_____
_____
_____
_____
_____
_____
_____
_____
_____

Things to Do

- [ ] _____
- [ ] _____
- [ ] _____
- [ ] _____
- [ ] _____
- [ ] _____
- [ ] _____
- [ ] _____
- [ ] _____
- [ ] _____
- [ ] _____
- [ ] _____

Notes

_____

_____

_____

_____

_____

_____

_____

_____

_____

Things to Do

- [ ] _____
- [ ] _____
- [ ] _____
- [ ] _____
- [ ] _____
- [ ] _____
- [ ] _____
- [ ] _____
- [ ] _____
- [ ] _____
- [ ] _____
- [ ] _____

Notes

_____
_____
_____
_____
_____
_____
_____
_____
_____

Things to Do

- [ ]
- [ ]
- [ ]
- [ ]
- [ ]
- [ ]
- [ ]
- [ ]
- [ ]
- [ ]
- [ ]
- [ ]

Notes

Things to Do

☐ _____
☐ _____
☐ _____
☐ _____
☐ _____
☐ _____
☐ _____
☐ _____
☐ _____
☐ _____
☐ _____
☐ _____

Notes

_____
_____
_____
_____
_____
_____
_____
_____
_____

Things to Do

- [ ] _____
- [ ] _____
- [ ] _____
- [ ] _____
- [ ] _____
- [ ] _____
- [ ] _____
- [ ] _____
- [ ] _____
- [ ] _____
- [ ] _____
- [ ] _____

Notes

_____

_____

_____

_____

_____

_____

_____

_____

_____

Things to Do

- [ ] _____
- [ ] _____
- [ ] _____
- [ ] _____
- [ ] _____
- [ ] _____
- [ ] _____
- [ ] _____
- [ ] _____
- [ ] _____
- [ ] _____
- [ ] _____

Notes

_____

_____

_____

_____

_____

_____

_____

_____

Things to Do

- [ ] _____
- [ ] _____
- [ ] _____
- [ ] _____
- [ ] _____
- [ ] _____
- [ ] _____
- [ ] _____
- [ ] _____
- [ ] _____
- [ ] _____
- [ ] _____

Notes

_____

_____

_____

_____

_____

_____

_____

_____

_____

Things to Do

- [ ] _____
- [ ] _____
- [ ] _____
- [ ] _____
- [ ] _____
- [ ] _____
- [ ] _____
- [ ] _____
- [ ] _____
- [ ] _____
- [ ] _____
- [ ] _____

Notes

_____

_____

_____

_____

_____

_____

_____

_____

Things to Do

- [ ] _____
- [ ] _____
- [ ] _____
- [ ] _____
- [ ] _____
- [ ] _____
- [ ] _____
- [ ] _____
- [ ] _____
- [ ] _____
- [ ] _____
- [ ] _____

Notes

_____

_____

_____

_____

_____

_____

_____

_____

_____

Things to Do

☐ _____
☐ _____
☐ _____
☐ _____
☐ _____
☐ _____
☐ _____
☐ _____
☐ _____
☐ _____
☐ _____
☐ _____

Notes

_____
_____
_____
_____
_____
_____
_____
_____
_____

Things to Do

☐ _____
☐ _____
☐ _____
☐ _____
☐ _____
☐ _____
☐ _____
☐ _____
☐ _____
☐ _____
☐ _____
☐ _____

Notes

_____
_____
_____
_____
_____
_____
_____
_____
_____

Things to Do

- [ ] _____
- [ ] _____
- [ ] _____
- [ ] _____
- [ ] _____
- [ ] _____
- [ ] _____
- [ ] _____
- [ ] _____
- [ ] _____
- [ ] _____
- [ ] _____

Notes

_____
_____
_____
_____
_____
_____
_____
_____
_____

Things to Do

- [ ] _____
- [ ] _____
- [ ] _____
- [ ] _____
- [ ] _____
- [ ] _____
- [ ] _____
- [ ] _____
- [ ] _____
- [ ] _____
- [ ] _____
- [ ] _____

Notes

_____

_____

_____

_____

_____

_____

_____

_____

_____

_____

Things to Do

- [ ]
- [ ]
- [ ]
- [ ]
- [ ]
- [ ]
- [ ]
- [ ]
- [ ]
- [ ]
- [ ]
- [ ]

Notes

Things to Do

- [ ]
- [ ]
- [ ]
- [ ]
- [ ]
- [ ]
- [ ]
- [ ]
- [ ]
- [ ]
- [ ]
- [ ]

Notes

Things to Do

☐ _____
☐ _____
☐ _____
☐ _____
☐ _____
☐ _____
☐ _____
☐ _____
☐ _____
☐ _____
☐ _____
☐ _____

Notes

_____
_____
_____
_____
_____
_____
_____
_____
_____

Things to Do

- [ ]
- [ ]
- [ ]
- [ ]
- [ ]
- [ ]
- [ ]
- [ ]
- [ ]
- [ ]
- [ ]
- [ ]

Notes

Calendars

2013

JANUARY
S	M	T	W	T	F	S
		1	2	3	4	5
6	7	8	9	10	11	12
13	14	15	16	17	18	19
20	21	22	23	24	25	26
27	28	29	30	31		

FEBRUARY
S	M	T	W	T	F	S
					1	2
3	4	5	6	7	8	9
10	11	12	13	14	15	16
17	18	19	20	21	22	23
24	25	26	27	28		

MARCH
S	M	T	W	T	F	S
					1	2
3	4	5	6	7	8	9
10	11	12	13	14	15	16
17	18	19	20	21	22	23
24	25	26	27	28	29	30
31						

APRIL
S	M	T	W	T	F	S
	1	2	3	4	5	6
7	8	9	10	11	12	13
14	15	16	17	18	19	20
21	22	23	24	25	26	27
28	29	30				

MAY
S	M	T	W	T	F	S
			1	2	3	4
5	6	7	8	9	10	11
12	13	14	15	16	17	18
19	20	21	22	23	24	25
26	27	28	29	30	31	

JUNE
S	M	T	W	T	F	S
						1
2	3	4	5	6	7	8
9	10	11	12	13	14	15
16	17	18	19	20	21	22
23	24	25	26	27	28	29
30						

JULY
S	M	T	W	T	F	S
	1	2	3	4	5	6
7	8	9	10	11	12	13
14	15	16	17	18	19	20
21	22	23	24	25	26	27
28	29	30	31			

AUGUST
S	M	T	W	T	F	S
				1	2	3
4	5	6	7	8	9	10
11	12	13	14	15	16	17
18	19	20	21	22	23	24
25	26	27	28	29	30	31

SEPTEMBER
S	M	T	W	T	F	S
1	2	3	4	5	6	7
8	9	10	11	12	13	14
15	16	17	18	19	20	21
22	23	24	25	26	27	28
29	30					

OCTOBER
S	M	T	W	T	F	S
		1	2	3	4	5
6	7	8	9	10	11	12
13	14	15	16	17	18	19
20	21	22	23	24	25	26
27	28	29	30	31		

NOVEMBER
S	M	T	W	T	F	S
					1	2
3	4	5	6	7	8	9
10	11	12	13	14	15	16
17	18	19	20	21	22	23
24	25	26	27	28	29	30

DECEMBER
S	M	T	W	T	F	S
1	2	3	4	5	6	7
8	9	10	11	12	13	14
15	16	17	18	19	20	21
22	23	24	25	26	27	28
29	30	31				

2014

JANUARY
S	M	T	W	T	F	S
			1	2	3	4
5	6	7	8	9	10	11
12	13	14	15	16	17	18
19	20	21	22	23	24	25
26	27	28	29	30	31	

FEBRUARY
S	M	T	W	T	F	S
						1
2	3	4	5	6	7	8
9	10	11	12	13	14	15
16	17	18	19	20	21	22
23	24	25	26	27	28	

MARCH
S	M	T	W	T	F	S
						1
2	3	4	5	6	7	8
9	10	11	12	13	14	15
16	17	18	19	20	21	22
23	24	25	26	27	28	29
30	31					

APRIL
S	M	T	W	T	F	S
		1	2	3	4	5
6	7	8	9	10	11	12
13	14	15	16	17	18	19
20	21	22	23	24	25	26
27	28	29	30			

MAY
S	M	T	W	T	F	S
				1	2	3
4	5	6	7	8	9	10
11	12	13	14	15	16	17
18	19	20	21	22	23	24
25	26	27	28	29	30	31

JUNE
S	M	T	W	T	F	S
1	2	3	4	5	6	7
8	9	10	11	12	13	14
15	16	17	18	19	20	21
22	23	24	25	26	27	28
29	30					

JULY
S	M	T	W	T	F	S
		1	2	3	4	5
6	7	8	9	10	11	12
13	14	15	16	17	18	19
20	21	22	23	24	25	26
27	28	29	30	31		

AUGUST
S	M	T	W	T	F	S
					1	2
3	4	5	6	7	8	9
10	11	12	13	14	15	16
17	18	19	20	21	22	23
24	25	26	27	28	29	30
31						

SEPTEMBER
S	M	T	W	T	F	S
	1	2	3	4	5	6
7	8	9	10	11	12	13
14	15	16	17	18	19	20
21	22	23	24	25	26	27
28	29	30				

OCTOBER
S	M	T	W	T	F	S
			1	2	3	4
5	6	7	8	9	10	11
12	13	14	15	16	17	18
19	20	21	22	23	24	25
26	27	28	29	30	31	

NOVEMBER
S	M	T	W	T	F	S
						1
2	3	4	5	6	7	8
9	10	11	12	13	14	15
16	17	18	19	20	21	22
23	24	25	26	27	28	29
30						

DECEMBER
S	M	T	W	T	F	S
	1	2	3	4	5	6
7	8	9	10	11	12	13
14	15	16	17	18	19	20
21	22	23	24	25	26	27
28	29	30	31			

2 0 1 5

JANUARY
S	M	T	W	T	F	S
				1	2	3
4	5	6	7	8	9	10
11	12	13	14	15	16	17
18	19	20	21	22	23	24
25	26	27	28	29	30	31

FEBRUARY
S	M	T	W	T	F	S
1	2	3	4	5	6	7
8	9	10	11	12	13	14
15	16	17	18	19	20	21
22	23	24	25	26	27	28

MARCH
S	M	T	W	T	F	S
1	2	3	4	5	6	7
8	9	10	11	12	13	14
15	16	17	18	19	20	21
22	23	24	25	26	27	28
29	30	31				

APRIL
S	M	T	W	T	F	S
			1	2	3	4
5	6	7	8	9	10	11
12	13	14	15	16	17	18
19	20	21	22	23	24	25
26	27	28	29	30		

MAY
S	M	T	W	T	F	S
					1	2
3	4	5	6	7	8	9
10	11	12	13	14	15	16
17	18	19	20	21	22	23
24	25	26	27	28	29	30
31						

JUNE
S	M	T	W	T	F	S
	1	2	3	4	5	6
7	8	9	10	11	12	13
14	15	16	17	18	19	20
21	22	23	24	25	26	27
28	29	30				

JULY
S	M	T	W	T	F	S
			1	2	3	4
5	6	7	8	9	10	11
12	13	14	15	16	17	18
19	20	21	22	23	24	25
26	27	28	29	30	31	

AUGUST
S	M	T	W	T	F	S
						1
2	3	4	5	6	7	8
9	10	11	12	13	14	15
16	17	18	19	20	21	22
23	24	25	26	27	28	29
30	31					

SEPTEMBER
S	M	T	W	T	F	S
		1	2	3	4	5
6	7	8	9	10	11	12
13	14	15	16	17	18	19
20	21	22	23	24	25	26
27	28	29	30			

OCTOBER
S	M	T	W	T	F	S
				1	2	3
4	5	6	7	8	9	10
11	12	13	14	15	16	17
18	19	20	21	22	23	24
25	26	27	28	29	30	31

NOVEMBER
S	M	T	W	T	F	S
1	2	3	4	5	6	7
8	9	10	11	12	13	14
15	16	17	18	19	20	21
22	23	24	25	26	27	28
29	30					

DECEMBER
S	M	T	W	T	F	S
		1	2	3	4	5
6	7	8	9	10	11	12
13	14	15	16	17	18	19
20	21	22	23	24	25	26
27	28	29	30	31		

2 0 1 6

JANUARY
S	M	T	W	T	F	S
					1	2
3	4	5	6	7	8	9
10	11	12	13	14	15	16
17	18	19	20	21	22	23
24	25	26	27	28	29	30
31						

FEBRUARY
S	M	T	W	T	F	S
	1	2	3	4	5	6
7	8	9	10	11	12	13
14	15	16	17	18	19	20
21	22	23	24	25	26	27
28	29					

MARCH
S	M	T	W	T	F	S
		1	2	3	4	5
6	7	8	9	10	11	12
13	14	15	16	17	18	19
20	21	22	23	24	25	26
27	28	29	30	31		

APRIL
S	M	T	W	T	F	S
					1	2
3	4	5	6	7	8	9
10	11	12	13	14	15	16
17	18	19	20	21	22	23
24	25	26	27	28	29	30

MAY
S	M	T	W	T	F	S
1	2	3	4	5	6	7
8	9	10	11	12	13	14
15	16	17	18	19	20	21
22	23	24	25	26	27	28
29	30	31				

JUNE
S	M	T	W	T	F	S
			1	2	3	4
5	6	7	8	9	10	11
12	13	14	15	16	17	18
19	20	21	22	23	24	25
26	27	28	29	30		

JULY
S	M	T	W	T	F	S
					1	2
3	4	5	6	7	8	9
10	11	12	13	14	15	16
17	18	19	20	21	22	23
24	25	26	27	28	29	30
31						

AUGUST
S	M	T	W	T	F	S
	1	2	3	4	5	6
7	8	9	10	11	12	13
14	15	16	17	18	19	20
21	22	23	24	25	26	27
28	29	30	31			

SEPTEMBER
S	M	T	W	T	F	S
				1	2	3
4	5	6	7	8	9	10
11	12	13	14	15	16	17
18	19	20	21	22	23	24
25	26	27	28	29	30	

OCTOBER
S	M	T	W	T	F	S
						1
2	3	4	5	6	7	8
9	10	11	12	13	14	15
16	17	18	19	20	21	22
23	24	25	26	27	28	29
30	31					

NOVEMBER
S	M	T	W	T	F	S
		1	2	3	4	5
6	7	8	9	10	11	12
13	14	15	16	17	18	19
20	21	22	23	24	25	26
27	28	29	30			

DECEMBER
S	M	T	W	T	F	S
				1	2	3
4	5	6	7	8	9	10
11	12	13	14	15	16	17
18	19	20	21	22	23	24
25	26	27	28	29	30	31

Calendars

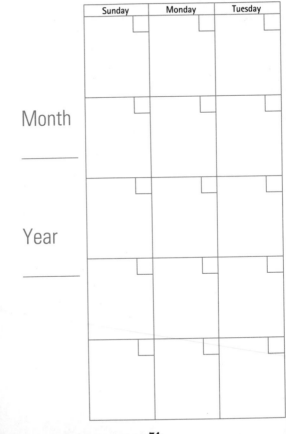

Month

_____

Year

_____

Sunday	Monday	Tuesday

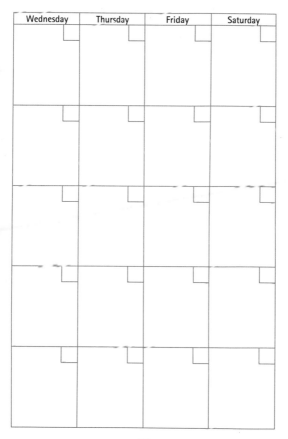

Wednesday	Thursday	Friday	Saturday

Month

_____

Year

_____

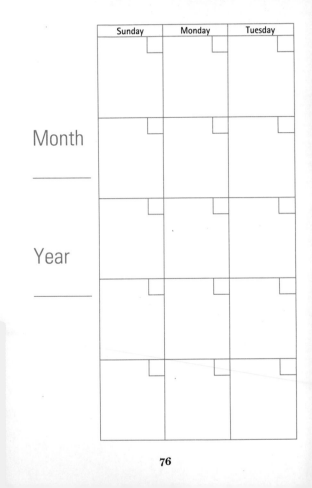

Sunday	Monday	Tuesday

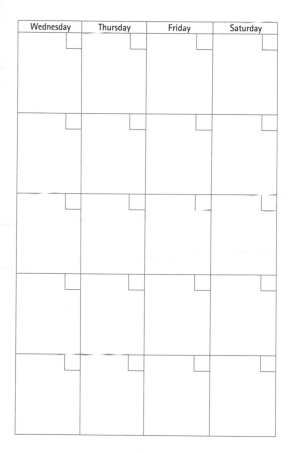

Wednesday	Thursday	Friday	Saturday

Calendars

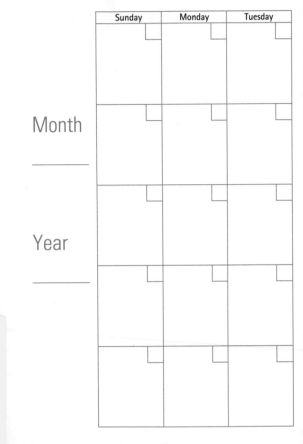

Month

_____

Year

_____

Sunday	Monday	Tuesday

Wednesday	Thursday	Friday	Saturday

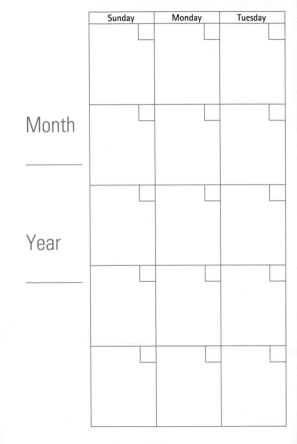

Month

_____

Year

_____

Sunday	Monday	Tuesday

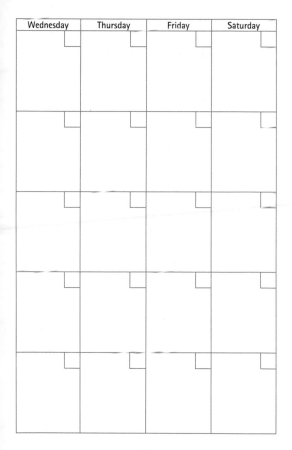

Wednesday	Thursday	Friday	Saturday

Calendars

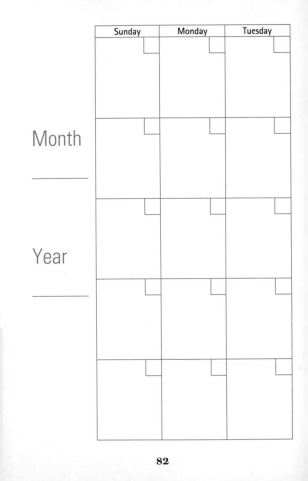

Month

_____

Year

_____

Sunday	Monday	Tuesday

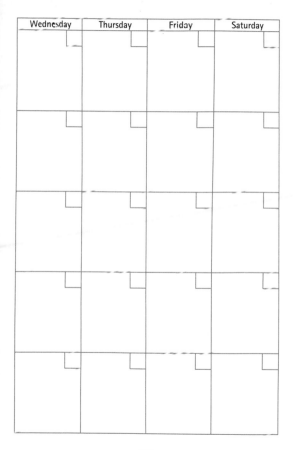

Wednesday	Thursday	Friday	Saturday

Calendars

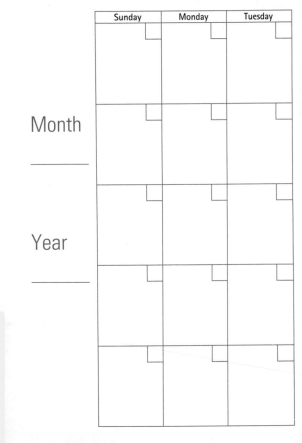

Month

_____

Year

_____

Sunday	Monday	Tuesday

Wednesday	Thursday	Friday	Saturday

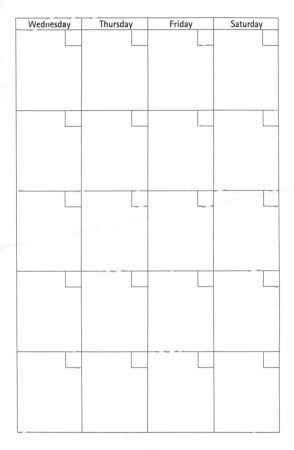

Calendars

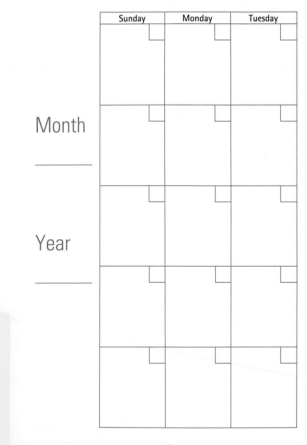

Month

_____

Year

_____

Sunday	Monday	Tuesday

Wednesday	Thursday	Friday	Saturday

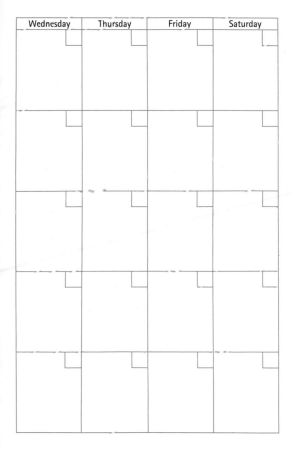

Calendars

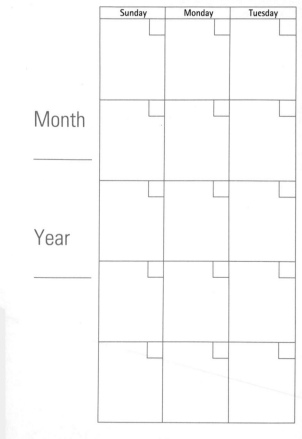

Month

_____

Year

_____

Sunday	Monday	Tuesday

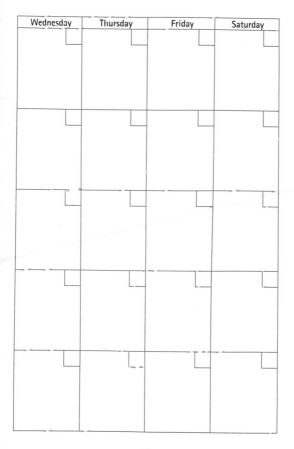

Wednesday	Thursday	Friday	Saturday

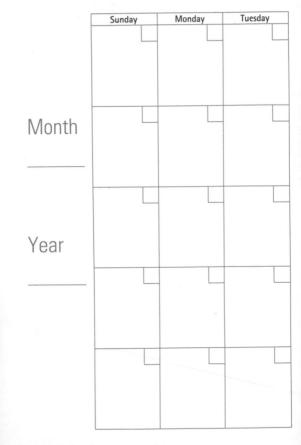

Month

_____

Year

_____

Sunday	Monday	Tuesday

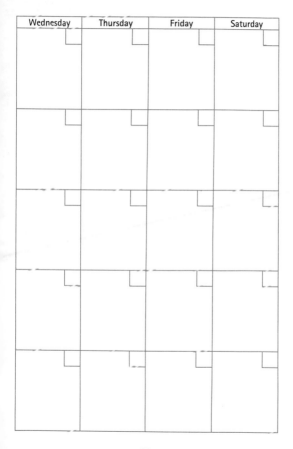

Wednesday	Thursday	Friday	Saturday

Calendars

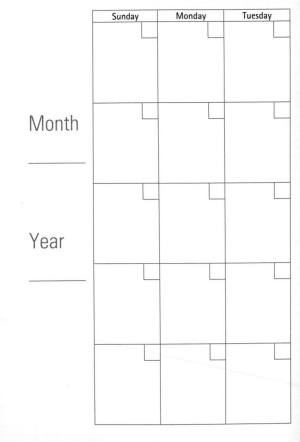

Month
_____

Year
_____

Sunday	Monday	Tuesday

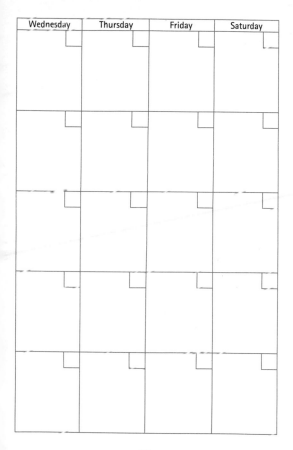

Wednesday	Thursday	Friday	Saturday

Calendars

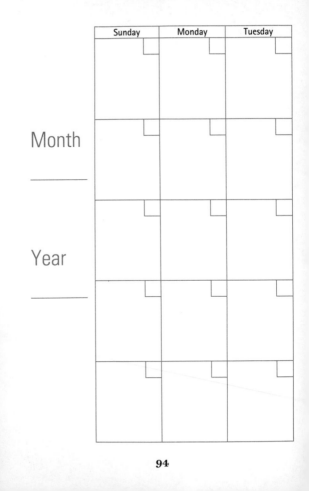

Sunday	Monday	Tuesday

Month
____

Year
____

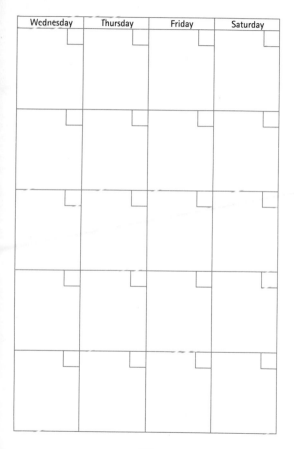

Wednesday	Thursday	Friday	Saturday

Calendars

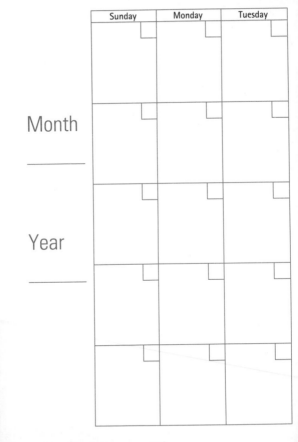

Month

_____

Year

_____

Sunday	Monday	Tuesday

Wednesday	Thursday	Friday	Saturday

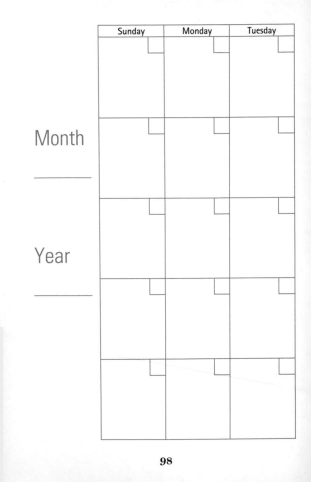

Month

———

Year

———

Sunday	Monday	Tuesday

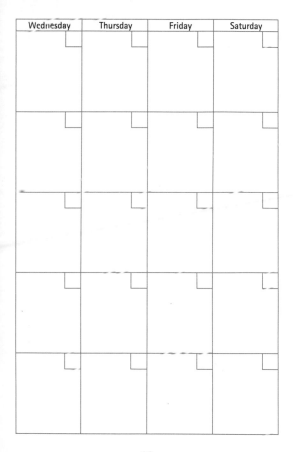

Wednesday	Thursday	Friday	Saturday

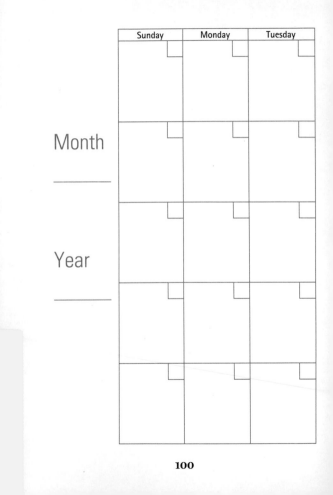

Month

_____

Year

_____

Sunday	Monday	Tuesday

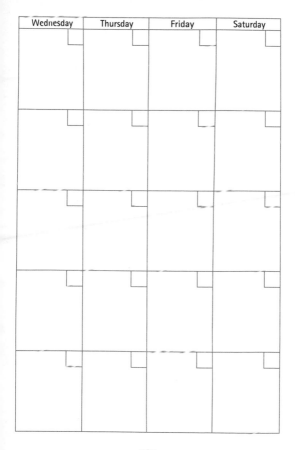

Wednesday	Thursday	Friday	Saturday

Calendars

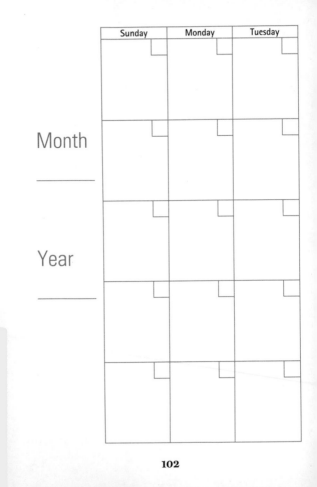

Sunday	Monday	Tuesday

Month

_____

Year

_____

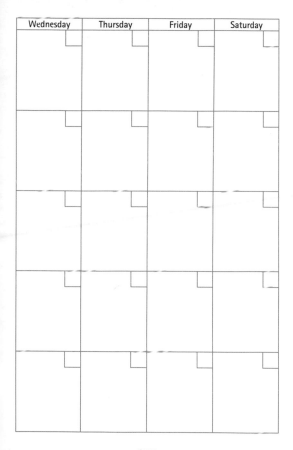

Wednesday	Thursday	Friday	Saturday

Calendars

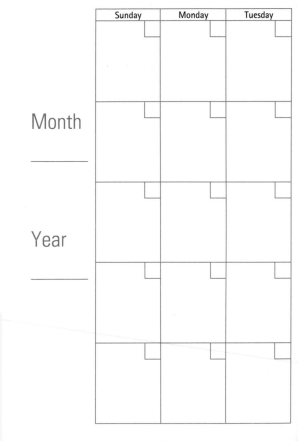

Month

_____

Year

_____

Sunday	Monday	Tuesday

Wednesday	Thursday	Friday	Saturday

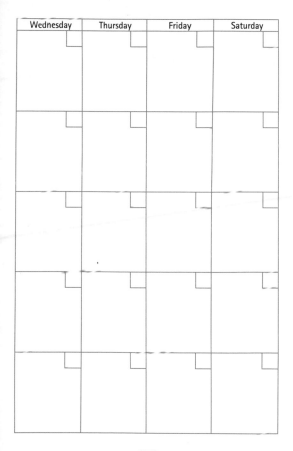

Calendars

Contacts

Wedding Consultant:

Company:

Address:

Phone:

E-mail:

Wedding day contact #:

Officiant:

Address:

Phone:

E-mail:

Wedding day contact #:

Ceremony Site:

Contact person:

Address:

Phone:

E-mail:

Wedding day contact #:

Reception Site:

Contact person:

Address:

Phone:

E-mail:

Wedding day contact #:

Caterer/Banquet Manager:

Company:

Address:

Phone:

E-mail:

Wedding day contact #:

Baker/Cake Decorator:

Company:

Address:

Phone:

E-mail:

Wedding day contact #:

Ceremony Musicians:

Company:

Address:

Phone:

E-mail:

Wedding day contact #:

Agency:

Contact person:

Phone:

E-mail:

Wedding day contact #:

Band/Disc Jockey:

Company:

Address:

Phone:

E-mail:

Wedding day contact #:

Agency:

Contact person:

Phone:

E-mail:

Wedding day contact #:

Florist:

Company:

Address:

Phone:

E-mail:

Wedding day contact #:

Photographer:

Company:

Address:

Phone:

E-mail:

Wedding day contact #:

Agency:

Contact person:

Phone:

E-mail:

Wedding day contact #:

Videographer:

Company:

Address:

Phone:

E-mail:

Wedding day contact #:

Agency:

Contact person:

Phone:

E-mail:

Wedding day contact #:

Rental Company:

Contact person:

Address:

Phone:

E-mail:

Wedding day contact #:

Bridal Salon:

Sales associate:

Address:

Phone:

E-mail:

Wedding day contact #:

(for seamstress if coming to bustle)

Bridesmaid Dress Source:

Contact person:

Address:

Phone:

E-mail:

Wedding day contact #:

Hairstylist:

Salon:

Address:

Phone:

E-mail:

Wedding day contact #:

Makeup Artist:

Salon:

Address:

Phone:

E-mail:

Wedding day contact #:

Transportation Service:

Contact person:

Address:

Phone:

E-mail:

Wedding day contact #:

Hotel #1:

Contact person:

Address:

Phone:

E-mail:

Reservation code:

Hotel #2:

Contact person:

Address:

Phone:

E-mail:

Reservation code:

Hotel #3:

Contact person:

Address:

Phone:

E-mail:

Reservation code:

Bridal Registry #1:

Contact person:

Address:

Phone:

E-mail:

Website:

Password:

Bridal Registry #2:

Contact person: _____

Address: _____

_____

Phone: _____

E-mail: _____

Website: _____

Password: _____

Bridal Registry #3:

Contact person: _____

Address: _____

_____

Phone: _____

E-mail: _____

Website: _____

Password: _____

Bridesmaid:

Address: _____

_____

Phone: _____

E-mail: _____

Wedding day contact #: _____

Bridesmaid:

Address:

Phone:

E-mail:

Wedding day contact #:

Bridesmaid:

Address:

Phone:

E-mail:

Wedding day contact #:

Bridesmaid:

Address:

Phone:

E-mail:

Wedding day contact #:

Bridesmaid:

Address:

Phone:

E-mail:

Wedding day contact #:

Bridesmaid:

Address:

Phone:

E-mail:

Wedding day contact #:

Bridesmaid:

Address:

Phone:

E-mail:

Wedding day contact #:

Groomsman:

Address:

Phone:

E-mail:

Wedding day contact #:

Groomsman:

Address:

Phone:

E-mail:

Wedding day contact #:

Groomsman:

Address:

Phone:

E-mail:

Wedding day contact #:

Groomsman:

Address:

Phone:

E-mail:

Wedding day contact #:

Groomsman:

Address:

Phone:

E-mail:

Wedding day contact #:

Groomsman:

Address:

Phone:

E-mail:

Wedding day contact #:

Groomsman:

Address:

Phone:

E-mail:

Wedding day contact #:

Usher:

Address:

Phone:

E mail:

Wedding day contact #:

Usher:

Address:

Phone:

E-mail:

Wedding day contact #:

Usher:

Address:

Phone:

E-mail:

Wedding day contact #:

Usher:

Address:

Phone:

E-mail:

Wedding day contact #:

Reader/Singer:

Address:

Phone:

E-mail:

Wedding day contact #:

Reader/Singer:

Address:

Phone:

E-mail:

Wedding day contact #:

Reader/Singer:

Address:

Phone:

E-mail:

Wedding day contact #:

Child Attendant:

Parents:

Address:

Phone:

E-mail:

Wedding day contact #:

Child Attendant:

Parents:

Address:

Phone:

E-mail:

Wedding day contact #:

Bride's Parents

Name:

Address:

Phone:

E-mail:

Wedding day contact #:

Name:

Address:

Phone:

E-mail:

Wedding day contact #:

Groom's Parents

Name:

Address:

Phone:

E-mail:

Wedding day contact #:

Name:

Address:

Phone:

E-mail:

Wedding day contact #:

Other Important People

Name:

Company:

Address:

Phone:

E-mail:

Wedding day contact #:

Name: _____

Company: _____

Address: _____

_____

Phone: _____

E-mail: _____

Wedding day contact #: _____

Name: _____

Company: _____

Address: _____

_____

Phone: _____

E-mail: _____

Wedding day contact #: _____

Name: _____

Company: _____

Address: _____

_____

Phone: _____

E-mail: _____

Wedding day contact #: _____

Bridesmaids' Measurements

Name:

| Bust: | Hips: |
| Waist: | Height: |

Name:

| Bust: | Hips: |
| Waist: | Height: |

Name:

| Bust: | Hips: |
| Waist: | Height: |

Name:

| Bust: | Hips: |
| Waist: | Height: |

Name:

| Bust: | Hips: |
| Waist: | Height: |

Name:

| Bust: | Hips: |
| Waist: | Height: |

Name:

| Bust: | Hips: |
| Waist: | Height: |